Stress
Management

Perspectives on Mental Health

by Susan R. Gregson

Consultant:
Geneva Riley, MSW, LCSW
Director, Primary Care Outreach
National Mental Health Association

LifeMatters
an imprint of Capstone Press
Mankato, Minnesota

LifeMatters Books are published by Capstone Press
PO Box 669 • 151 Good Counsel Drive • Mankato, Minnesota 56002
http://www.capstone-press.com

Printed in the United States of America

Library of Congress Cataloging-in-Publication Data
Gregson, Susan R.
     Stress management / by Susan R. Gregson.
         p.   cm. — (Perspectives on mental health)
     Includes bibliographical references and index.
     Summary: Explains what stress is, some causes, and various ways to handle stress and cope with its effects.
     ISBN 0-7368-0432-3 (book) — ISBN 0-7368-0440-4 (series)
     1. Stress in adolescence—Juvenile literature. 2. Stress management for teenagers—Juvenile literature. [1. Stress (Psychology)] I. Title. II. Series.
     BF724.3.S86 G74 2000
     155.9′042—dc21

                                            99-056217
                                          CIP

Staff Credits
Marta Fahrenz, editor; Adam Lazar, designer; Jodi Theisen, photo researcher

Photo Credits
Cover: ©Capstone Press/Adam Lazar
FPG International/©John Terence Turner, 25; ©100% Rag Productions, 33; ©Stephen Rausser, 36; ©Jim Cummins, 45; ©Elizabeth Simpson, 46; ©Bruce Byers, 47
Index Stock Photography/©Myrleen Cate, 39; 59
International Stock/©Scott Thode, 15; ©Lynn St. John, 54
Unicorn Stock Photos/©Steve Bourgeois, 14; ©Maggie Finefrock, 26; ©Eric R. Berndt, 42; ©Jeff Greenberg, 51
Uniphoto/6, 16
Visuals Unlimited/©Jeff Greenberg, 10

A 0 9 8 7 6 5 4 3 2 1

Table of Contents

Chapter Overview

Stress is a reaction of the body and mind to change.

Things that cause stress are called stressors. They can be internal or external. Internal stressors are feelings that cause stress. External stressors are things outside a person that cause stress.

Stress is normal. Some types of stress can be good for you. However, certain kinds of stress can be unhealthy.

Chronic or ongoing stress can cause serious health problems.

Everyone has stress at times. It is important to learn how to reduce stress and deal with its effects.

Chapter 1

What Is Stress?

"Your face is white as a ghost," Taylor tells her friend

WHITNEY, AGE 16

Whitney. "What's wrong with you?" Whitney tells her that last night she overheard her parents talking about getting a divorce. Whitney's heart begins to pound. Her hands are sweating and she feels dizzy. She has a lump in her throat. She tells Taylor that the more she thinks about her parents' conversation, the sicker she feels. The bell rings for class and Whitney groans. She has a math test in two minutes and she didn't study last night. She feels her face get hot.

Stress is a person's reaction to change. It is a physical and mental response to feelings, situations, other people, or places. Whitney is feeling and showing typical signs of stress.

The things that cause stress are called stressors. A stressor can be internal or external. An internal stressor is a feeling or emotion that causes stress. Whitney's fear of failing her math test is an internal stressor. An external stressor is something outside a person that causes stress. Her parents' possible divorce is an external stressor for Whitney.

Stressors can be minor, like misplacing your keys. Stressors also can be major. Examples of major stressors include the death of a family member or friend, loss of a job, or a relationship breakup.

Stress Management

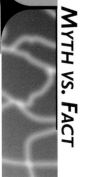

MYTH VS. FACT

Physical Reactions to Stress

When a person experiences stress, the brain releases chemicals called epinephrine and cortisol. Epinephrine is sometimes called adrenaline. A stressor sends these chemicals, or stress hormones, racing through the body.

Stress hormones prepare the body to protect itself from danger. The hormones signal blood to move to the heart and other organs. People experiencing stress might suddenly feel hot. Their heart may beat faster and their muscles may tense. Their hands and feet might feel cold or clammy. Their senses may become sharper. People might feel like they can smell, see, and taste things more clearly. Once the stressor disappears, the stress hormones quiet down. The body gradually goes back to normal.

More physical and mental reactions to stress are described in Chapter 3.

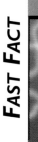

The Good and the Bad

Not all stress is bad. Stress can make life more exciting. It can motivate people to make a needed change or to figure out a problem.

LUCIA, AGE 13

Lucia wrote an essay for her English class. Her teacher thought it was so good that she entered the essay in a contest. Lucia's essay won second place. She was happy and excited when her teacher told her the good news. Then her stomach flopped when she heard she would have to read her essay at a ceremony. Ms. Gray told Lucia that she would help her practice reading the essay. Then Lucia might feel more comfortable in front of an audience. Lucia was nervous, but she also was thrilled about the $100 prize she had won. She knew her mom would be proud of her, too.

Here's what some teens report:

1. Want to be alone

2. Fight with brothers and sisters

3. Daydream

4. Bite nails

5. Have trouble sleeping

6. Cry easily

7. Lose interest in school and homework

8. Can't concentrate

Good Stress

Good stress can make a person feel both nervous and excited at the same time. Lucia was nervous about speaking in public. However, she was excited to have won a prize for her essay. Likewise, a person might look forward to going to a new school and making new friends. At the same time, the person might be worried about being liked or accepted. Good stress can cause a person to feel frightened or nervous. Like Lucia, it also can motivate a person to accomplish a difficult task or take on a challenging project. Experts sometimes call good stress *eustress*, or positive stress.

Bad Stress

Bad stress can cause a person to feel angry, scared, or sad. This type of stress can be unhealthy. A move to a new school can cause unhealthy stress if the person is upset about leaving good friends. He or she may feel too shy to make new friends. The person may feel like crying all the time. Unhealthy stress can cause people to feel constantly nervous and on edge. They may have stomachaches or headaches. Unhealthy stress also is called *dis-stress*, or negative stress.

Chronic Stress

Often stress is short term. It lasts only a little while. For example, missing the school bus usually is stressful only until you find another way to get to school. Once you are at school, you may even forget what happened.

Some people experience ongoing stress. This is called chronic stress. Events like a death or divorce in the family can cause chronic stress. Some people live in stressful environments, such as homes where alcohol or other drug abuse is present. These people also may experience chronic stress.

People with chronic stress have stress hormones that are working overtime. After a while, their body weakens and grows tired. These people may say they are burned out or stressed out. They might have stomach problems, headaches, or body pain. They may feel constantly depressed, anxious, or tired. Often they have poor eating habits. People with chronic stress may find it difficult to focus on day-to-day living. Chronic stress can lead to high blood pressure, heart problems, and stroke.

Stress is part of everyone's life. It is important to learn about the effects of stress and find ways to manage and reduce it. You can never completely eliminate stress from your life. However, you can learn to control it so that it doesn't control you.

Points to Consider

What are some of your internal stressors?

What are some of your external stressors?

Think about what happened last week. What events caused good stress? What events caused bad stress?

Do you know anyone who has chronic stress? What causes stress for that person?

Chapter
Overview

Chapter Overview

Many things cause stress. For teens, the main areas of stress are school, work, family, and fitting in with peers. Other areas of stress for teens are sexuality, the world, and their future.

Some people are better than others at handling stress. Experts call these people stress hardy.

Some teens are at risk for chronic stress. They may be depressed, have an unstable home life, or experience unexpected events.

Secondhand stress is a person's reaction to events that have not happened directly to him or her. Secondhand stress can cause the same reactions as stress.

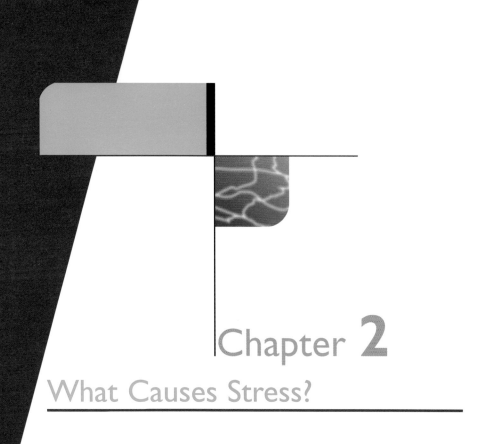

Chapter **2**

What Causes Stress?

Teens and Stress

Many things create stress in a teen's life. Some are small, like fighting with a brother or sister over what to watch on television. Others are more serious, like failing a test or crunching the fender of the family car. Overall, experts identify several main areas that cause teens stress. They are school, work, family, fitting in with peers, sexuality, the world, and the teen's future.

School

School is a stressor for many teens. They worry about their grades. They may struggle with homework and passing tests. Many feel they must meet the expectations of parents and teachers. This can cause more stress. Teens who play sports might feel the pressure of being part of a team. They may worry about how they'll perform in front of teammates and classmates. They may fear letting their teammates down if they don't play well.

Work

Teens who have an after-school job often feel stress. They might be expected to work long hours. The job might be physically demanding. Some jobs can be boring and repetitive for teens. If they work with customers, they may have to solve problems or deal with angry people.

Some teens must work to contribute to the family income. They may feel like they work so much that they don't have time for schoolwork or friends.

Family

A source of many teens' stress is getting along with a parent or caregiver. The teen years are a time when many teens want to be independent. They feel ready to make their own decisions. A teen may disagree with parents' rules and rebel. These situations can cause stress for parents and teens alike.

Chronic illness of a parent or other family member can be difficult for everyone in the family. Death of a family member can cause deeply painful feelings. Parents' divorce or separation is a frequent cause of teen stress. Other family issues that cause stress are described later in this chapter.

Fitting in With Peers

Most teens feel stress about fitting in with their peers. For many teens, peer pressure causes stress. Peer pressure occurs when peers ask someone to do, say, or try something that may make that person uncomfortable. For example, you might be afraid your friends won't like you if you refuse to drink alcohol.

Some teens are teased for the clothes they wear or the way they look. Being teased can be painful and embarrassing. People who are bullied may not want to go to school because they are scared, depressed, or angry. Peer pressure can be a powerful stressor.

Sexuality

Many people begin exploring their sexuality for the first time in their teen years. Most people are attracted to members of the opposite sex. This is called heterosexuality. Some teens might be attracted to members of the same sex. This is called homosexuality. Males who are attracted to other males are called gay. Females who are attracted to other females are called lesbian. People who are attracted to both males and females are called bisexual.

Gay, lesbian, and bisexual teens often feel alone and misunderstood. Classmates may treat them badly. Family and friends might be upset with them. These teens can experience more stress than their heterosexual friends.

The World and the Future

Teens often are anxious about things that happen in the world around them. They may worry about crime and the environment.

Many teens are concerned about their future. They may wonder what kind of job they will have and what kind of relationships they will experience. They may worry about going to college or technical school. Anxiety about the future is a common stressor in teens because their life can take so many directions.

Andy worries about what will
happen after graduation. His   *ANDY, AGE 17*
mother thinks he should be looking at colleges. But he loves
his part-time job at the auto shop and wants to keep working
there. He'd like to work there full time and earn enough
money to get his own place. Andy keeps putting off his
decisions. The future seems too overwhelming to even think
about.

Rolling With the Punches or Falling Apart at the Seams

Some teens seem to handle stress as it comes along and move on
with their life. Experts say these people are stress hardy. They
naturally handle stress well. They can deal with many stressors
without becoming ill. Stress-hardy people usually have high self-
esteem, which means they feel good about themselves. People
with high self-esteem often discuss and solve problems as they
come up. They are confident about making decisions.

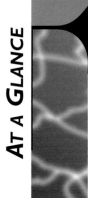
One survey showed that the top five signs of stress for young people are:

Insomnia, or inability to sleep

Stomachaches

Sick feeling

Headaches

Restlessness

Other people seem to fall apart when they experience stress. For these people, stressors pile up until they feel like they can't handle one more thing. These people might have low self-esteem. They may feel like they can't do anything right and that only bad things happen to them. They often find it hard to cope with change. Many cannot talk with others about their feelings. This may be their greatest obstacle in dealing with stress. Talking about their feelings can be like letting off steam. It can keep stress from boiling over and taking control of their life.

When Stress Hits Hardest

Some teens feel overwhelmed by stress because of other things going on in their life. They may be depressed. Some may live in families where stress is constant. Some may be separated from their family. Others may experience upsetting events.

Depression

Stress can feel overwhelming to young people who are depressed. Everyone feels sad or blue once in a while. The feelings usually go away after a day or two. However, depression is a serious illness. A person with depression feels extremely sad, hopeless, or helpless. These feelings can go on for weeks or longer. A person with depression can feel overwhelmed and desperate with even a small amount of stress. People with depression often need professional help to get better.

Stress can affect whole families. Experts call this family stress. Money problems, a parent changing jobs, or a family member leaving home can lead to family stress.

Family Environment

It is not uncommon for teens to live in a home where family members frequently fight or don't get along. Some live in a home where a parent is ill and the teen must act as caregiver. Many families live in poverty. These circumstances can cause a teen to feel stressed.

Some teens live in a home where there is abuse of alcohol or other drugs. They may live with physical or sexual abuse or other violence. They may be removed from their home because of these situations. Such teens may be able to do little more than survive each day. Living in such a family environment can cause chronic stress.

Unexpected Events

Teens who experience unexpected major events also may find it difficult to manage stress. These events might include becoming pregnant, losing a job, or breaking up with a girlfriend or boyfriend. Death of a loved one can cause long-term stress. Even positive unexpected events, such as winning a scholarship, can cause a teen to feel anxious.

Stressful events have been linked to an increased risk of heart attack. For example, a greater number of heart attacks than usual occur in the days following an earthquake. Experts think the higher numbers might be related to the stress caused by the unexpected, frightening event.

Secondhand Stress

CHARIS, AGE 15

Charis couldn't keep her eyes off the TV. She was watching a story about three teens shot and killed in the hallway of a high school. Charis's cousin lived in the same community as the dead teenagers. The news was full of stories about the teens and the classmate who shot them. Charis was edgy and sad. She and her friends seemed to talk only about the shootings. They wondered if it could happen in their school. One morning Charis woke up crying. She did not want to go to school. She had a knot in her stomach and she threw up. She just knew someone would bring a gun to school that day.

Charis is experiencing secondhand stress. Something that has not happened directly to her is the cause of her stress. However, Charis wonders if the same thing might happen to her. She feels empathy with the victims' families and friends. She can feel their shock and sadness as if it were her own. She imagines how her own loved ones would feel if she were killed.

Secondhand stress causes the same symptoms as stress. Many people experience secondhand stress because so much information is instantly available through TV, newspapers, and other media. For example, after news of an airline crash, someone planning a trip may be anxious about flying in a plane. The person may fear the same thing might happen.

Points to Consider

Think of the main areas of stress for teens. Name a stressor you have from one of these areas.

Do you know someone who is stress hardy? How does that person deal with stress?

Think of some news that made you worry. How did you feel when you heard the news?

Whom can you talk with when you feel worried?

Chapter
Overview

The body reacts to stress with an automatic flight or fight response.

Stress causes short-term and long-term physical and emotional symptoms. Some short-term symptoms include a racing heart and sweaty palms. Two long-term symptoms are fatigue and changes in appetite.

A stress test can help determine if a person is experiencing unhealthy stress.

Chapter **3**
The Mind and Body Connection

Chapter 1 explained the body's physical reactions to stress. This chapter explains how the mind and body react together to stress.

Experts say humans' physical reactions to stress go back to prehistoric times. Early humans needed to react quickly to dangerous situations. Their stress hormones allowed them to outrun a hungry lion or ward off an angry mother bear. Stress hormones gave their body a power surge. They could run faster, see farther, and jump higher. Early humans depended on this flight or fight response to survive. This response physically prepares the person either to fight an enemy or to run away.

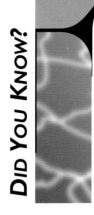

Exercise is one of the best ways to manage stress. Physical activity lowers the amount of cortisol in your blood. Cortisol is a stress hormone.

The Stress Response Today

Thousands of years later, the body still reacts to certain stressors with a flight or fight response. The mind tells the body to react to stress as if life depended on it. Within seconds of sudden stress, the heart races, the body sweats, and body systems start to shut down. Your stomach might gurgle or you might feel the urge to go to the bathroom. This urge is the body's way of ridding itself of excess weight so that it can move faster.

The body can easily handle the flight or fight response when it happens infrequently and lasts for a short time. Unfortunately, when a person has many stressors every day, the body begins to wear down. It doesn't have enough time between stressors to recover. The digestive system might break down, causing the person to get stomachaches and feel like vomiting. Headache pain may be constant. The person's immune system may weaken and fail to fight off disease and infection.

Ben just failed another math test. He is beginning to worry *BEN, AGE 18* that he will not graduate from high school this year. He will lose his track scholarship if he doesn't graduate. Ben's father scolds him for flunking the test. "Get out of my face!" Ben screams. He is dizzy and his mouth is dry. His hands are sweaty, too. Ben storms out of the room.

Stress Symptoms

When people react to stress, the mind and body show signs, or symptoms. Some last only a few minutes, while others can last a long time. These symptoms can be physical or emotional. Some of the symptoms of stress are listed in the chart on the following page.

Short-Term Symptoms of Stress	Long-Term Symptoms of Stress
Upset stomach, or feeling "butterflies"	Skin rash
Vomiting	Asthma
Racing heart	Frequent colds
Dizziness	Constant crying
Dry mouth	Self-blaming or loss of confidence
Sweaty hands	Loss of appetite or increased appetite
Tension and anxiety	Constant fatigue
Shaking	

Top 10 Ways to Reduce Stress

1. Exercise regularly.

2. Eat healthy foods.

3. Take time each day to relax.

4. Set aside time each day to spend with friends and family.

5. Laugh.

6. Be playful.

7. Don't plan too many activities in a day.

8. Treat others as you would like to be treated.

9. Don't put things off until the last minute.

10. Try not to worry about things you can't change.

When people have more stress than they can handle, they often have trouble getting along with others. They may be irritable and short-tempered. They may not be able to concentrate on school and work. Often people who are experiencing stress have trouble sleeping. They may lose their appetite or overeat.

Take a Stress Test

You may wonder about your own reactions to stress. The chart on the following page shows nine questions adapted from a list from the National Mental Health Association.

Are You Stressed?

Write your answer to each question on a sheet of paper.

1. Do little problems and disappointments upset you a lot?	YES	NO
2. Do little things in life fail to satisfy you?	YES	NO
3. Are you always thinking about your worries?	YES	NO
4. Do you feel like you never do anything right?	YES	NO
5. Are you always tired?	YES	NO
6. Do you get angry about things that did not used to bother you?	YES	NO
7. Have your sleeping habits changed? For example, are you sleeping more or less?	YES	NO
8. Have your appetite or eating habits changed? For example, are you eating more or less?	YES	NO
9. Do you have headaches, backaches, or other body pain frequently?	YES	NO

Add up the number of yes and no answers. If you answer yes to five or more questions, you may be experiencing too much stress.

A recent survey showed that 51 percent of Canadian teens ages 13 to 18 felt stressed. Stressful times ranged from once a month to all the time. More than half of the teens said school was their greatest stressor.

Fortunately, there are some simple ways to help reduce the effects of stress. These are described in the next chapter.

Points to Consider

Think of a time when you were suddenly stressed. How did your body react?

How do you feel when you are stressed? What are some of the thoughts that go through your head?

Have you ever experienced the flight or fight reaction to stress? What did you do?

Chapter Overview

Relaxation is one of the best ways to reduce stress. Some ways to relax include stretching, taking a walk, listening to music, or writing in a journal.

Deep breathing exercises help a person to relax and reduce stressors.

Sometimes relaxing can turn into a regular way to avoid or escape problems without solving them.

Other techniques to reduce stress include acupuncture, biofeedback, and herbal remedies.

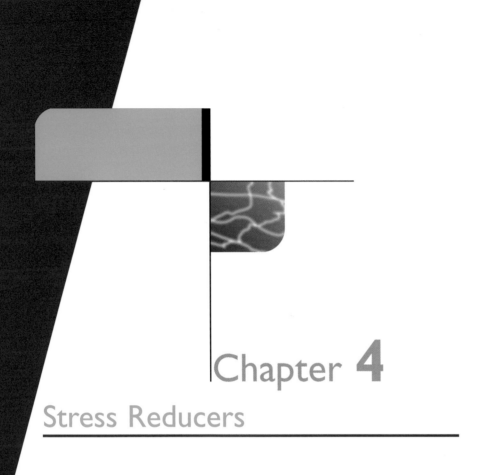

Chapter **4**

Stress Reducers

Relaxation: Turning Off the Stress Response

For years, experts have studied ways to turn off the stress response. Relaxation is one effective method. Relaxation can help a person escape stress temporarily. It can give the mind and body a break. Some people can relax so well that their pulse and breathing slows. Their blood pressure drops. Some experts call this the relaxation response. People can use their natural relaxation response to fight stress symptoms.

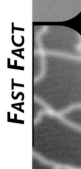

Research shows that massage can decrease the level of stress hormones in the blood and put people in a better mood.

Relaxation doesn't cost money. It just takes a little time. Some of the things you can do to relax and turn off the stress response are:

Stretch, change your posture, or squeeze a tennis ball.

Take a slow walk. Pay attention to your surroundings. Try not to think about anything except what you are seeing, smelling, hearing, and touching.

Listen to your favorite music.

Listen to a relaxation recording. These are audio recordings of soothing voices or nature sounds, such as the ocean or a rainstorm.

Take a hot bath.

Write about your feelings in a notebook or journal. Then put it away, close your eyes, and imagine your troubles floating from the pages.

Play a game, watch TV, or read a book.

Close your eyes and take a quick trip in your head to a favorite place.

Try not to think about anything else but the thing you are doing at the moment.

"It used to stress me out to talk in front of a class. A friend taught me this trick. She told me to 'see' myself standing in front of the class doing a great job. Now, whenever I give a report, I picture myself doing an awesome job. I still get a little nervous, but I don't get stressed out."—Blake, age 17

Take a Deep Breath

When people become stressed, their breathing is quick and shallow. However, when people are relaxed, their breathing is deep and slow. Deep breathing can help people relax and provides relief from stress. Here's how to do a deep breathing exercise:

Lie on your back on a padded floor or bed. Put your arms at your sides with palms up. Keep your legs straight and point your toes upward.

Close your eyes. Then close your mouth and breathe through your nose. Put your hand on the part of your chest that rises the most as you breathe in.

Put both hands on your stomach and breathe more slowly. Notice how your stomach rises and falls as you breathe in and out.

If your stomach is not moving very much, press your hand down as you breathe out and let it rise as you breathe in. Concentrate on breathing deeply in and out of your stomach, not your chest.

Clear your mind of all thought. If that is not possible, think about whatever pops into your head and think of only that thing.

Deep breathing in a quiet place while lying down is an effective way to ease stress. However, you can do deep breathing almost anywhere. Take deep, long breaths while standing in a checkout line or waiting in a traffic jam. This can help you instantly feel more calm.

If Relaxing Becomes an Escape

As soon as Jeanne gets home from school, she plops in front of **JEANNE, AGE 15** the television set. She never calls her friends or plays outside. If she is not watching TV, she plays video games. On Saturday mornings, her mom won't let her watch TV and asks her to go outside for fresh air. Jeanne goes back to bed instead and sleeps until the afternoon.

Watching TV, playing video games, or taking a nap can be a great way to escape from a stressful day. These activities help some people to relax, rest, and recover. However, sometimes they can turn into an escape from problems. They can be ways to run from stress instead of dealing with it. Friends or family members may tell you that you spend too much time on an activity. If so, try to limit your time doing that activity. Too much time in bed or watching TV might signal that you are trying to escape your problems. This could be a sign of depression, which was described in Chapter 2.

Depression is a treatable illness. Ask a parent, spiritual leader, or trusted adult for help if you think you may be depressed.

Other Ways to Reduce Stress

Other techniques to reduce stress include acupuncture, biofeedback, and herbal remedies. These therapies are different from traditional medicine in North America. Healers in some of these therapies are called practitioners. Patients may be called clients.

These techniques may help to lower stress and increase energy. Therapies such as herbal remedies should be used with a doctor's approval.

Acupuncture

Acupuncture is an ancient Chinese method of healing. Acupuncturists insert fine needles at specific points on the body. It is believed that this process changes the chemical balance of the body and reduces chronic pain and anxiety. Practitioners can be found in the phone book under *Acupuncture* or *Health Services.*

Biofeedback

In biofeedback, an electronic monitor is connected to the skin. The monitor measures heart rate, blood pressure, muscle tension, brain wave activity, and skin temperature. A trained practitioner interprets the information for the client. The aim is to help tense and anxious clients learn how to relax. Practitioners are listed in the phone book under headings such as *Biofeedback Therapists, Physicians/Psychiatrists, Psychologists,* or *Psychotherapists.*

Herbal Remedies

Medicinal herbs have been used throughout history. Some herbs that have been used to reduce tension and stress include bergamot, chamomile, lavender, and sandalwood. North American doctors do not usually prescribe herbs. Practitioners who offer herbal remedies can be found in the phone book under *Herbal Medicine, Chinese Medicine,* and *Naturopathy.*

Points to Consider

What three things did you do this week to relax?

What are some signs that a person may be avoiding his or her problems?

Do you think talking about your stressful experiences with others might be helpful? Why or why not?

Chapter Overview

Managing and reducing stress takes practice, but it can be done.

Knowing your limits, planning, taking care of yourself, and communicating are ways to help manage stress.

Many people need help dealing with stress at some point in their life. Don't be afraid to ask for help when you are feeling overwhelmed.

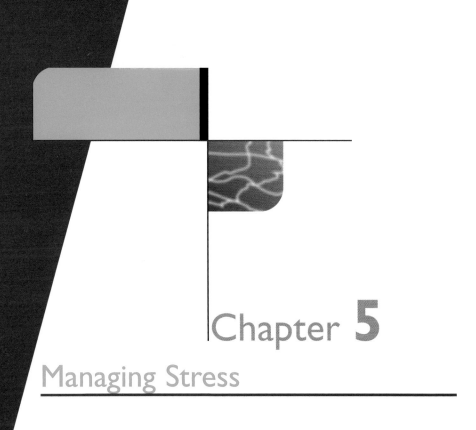

Chapter **5**

Managing Stress

Managing and reducing stress takes practice, but it can be done. Since stress is part of everyone's life, it makes sense to try to control it, reduce it, or deal with it. This chapter gives you some tips for managing the stress in your life.

Things that can help you manage your stress are knowing your limits, planning, taking care of yourself, and communicating with others.

Know Your Limits: Learn to Say No

Many people feel stressed because they take on more activities or responsibilities than they can handle. Sometimes learning to say no is the best stress reliever.

Teens today often complain about feeling overwhelmed with school, work, sports or clubs, and other activities. You may be surprised to learn that it is okay to say no. You don't have to attend every sporting event at school. You don't have to go out with your friends every Friday and Saturday night.

Feeling pressure and stress from having too much to do can be a vicious cycle. Many times people with a lot of responsibilities end up feeling like they can't do any of them well. This causes even more stress. Putting a limit on the activities you do can make your life less stressful and more manageable.

"Hey, Ray," called Jerome. "We're going over to Joe's Friday night to shoot some hoops. Then we're going to the game. Want to come?" Ray was exhausted. He had just turned in his history term paper. It had taken him all night to finish it. He planned to write a story for the school newspaper after he got home from work. All he wanted to do Friday night was fall asleep. "I think I'll pass," said Ray. "I want to, but I've just got too much going on right now." Ray felt bad for a few minutes after Jerome walked away. Then he felt a huge sense of relief. "That wasn't so bad," he thought. "Maybe I should say no more often."

Plan

Chapter 1 explained that stress is a reaction to change. Sometimes people become stressed when a situation changes and takes them by surprise. It's impossible to anticipate or plan for every situation in your life. However, taking time each day to think about what's ahead can reduce the chance of a stress-causing surprise.

"When I am feeling tense, I head outside for a walk, even in the rain or snow. It helps clear my head."
—Cetta, age 13

"I like to head outdoors to read a book under a tree, ride my bike, or fly a kite. My favorite winter stress buster is a wild snowball fight with my friends."
—Brian, age 14

SIRAH, AGE 15

Sirah lay in bed for a few minutes after the alarm went off. "Let's see," she thought. "What do I have to do today?" Suddenly she remembered. "I forgot to study for the chemistry quiz," she thought. "I knew I should have written it down on my calendar!" Sirah knew what she would be doing in study hall that morning.

Planning can help you have some control over what happens in your life. Thinking about and planning for the day's events can help you anticipate situations. Sirah was stressed when she realized that she forgot to study for the chemistry quiz. However, she would have felt a lot more stress if she had walked into class unprepared.

Planning can involve keeping lists of the things you have to do. It also can involve writing down daily goals in a journal or diary. Sometimes just taking time each day to think and write can help you feel organized and in control.

Take Care of Yourself

An important part of successfully managing stress is keeping strong and healthy both physically and mentally.

Exercise

Regular exercise helps get rid of tension and anxiety. Studies have shown that exercise provides a temporary release from stress. Exercise helps the body and mind recover from the effects of stressors. During exercise, the body releases endorphins. These chemicals are natural stress fighters and mood lifters. Experts recommend some form of exercise 15 to 30 minutes each day.

Eat Healthy Foods

Stress can affect digestion and the body's ability to absorb nutrients. The body needs these substances to be healthy. A well-nourished body is able to deal with the physical effects of stress. A balanced diet includes plenty of water, fruits, vegetables, protein, and whole grains. The Food Guide Pyramid can help you pick the right foods to eat. This pyramid is a widely accepted guide for helping people to eat a healthy diet. In Canada, the guide is presented as a rainbow. It is called Canada's Food Guide. Ask your doctor or school nurse for a copy.

Avoid Caffeine, Alcohol, Tobacco, and Other Drugs

Avoiding caffeine, a stimulant found in coffee and many soft drinks, can keep you more relaxed. Skip alcohol and other drugs, too. Caffeine, tobacco, alcohol, and other drugs can cause tension, nervousness, and anxiety. These effects are similar to the reactions caused by stress. Although many people think smoking helps them relax, tobacco actually stimulates the nervous system. Tobacco use deprives the body of oxygen.

Sleep

Stress is hard on the body's systems. A person needs adequate sleep for systems to recover from the effects of stress and other influences. Too little sleep weakens the immune system. This means you are less able to fight off disease and infection. Too little sleep may affect memory and coordination, which is the smooth working of muscles. Most teens need 8 to 10 hours of sleep each night.

Take a Break

Managing stress is easier when you are thinking clearly and calmly. It's important to take a break from situations that cause you stress. Take time each day to do something fun or relaxing. You could do a crossword puzzle, play a video game, or take a walk or a bike ride. Even short breaks can make you feel refreshed and better able to handle your stress.

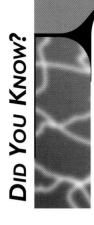

In situations of short-term stress, the senses usually become sharper. This is because the body is preparing itself for mental and physical challenges.

Communicate

An important key to managing stress is talking about it. Hiding your feelings or pretending something doesn't bother you when it does can make stress worse. Many people who stuff their stress become ill. A healthier way to deal with stress is to figure out what is causing the stress and then talk about it.

TERRY AND BRAD, AGE 16

Terry was always broke. Whenever he and Brad went out for a burger, Brad always ended up paying. "Sorry, man, I forgot my wallet," Terry would say. Or, "I'm a little short this week. I'll treat next time." He never paid Brad back either.

Brad couldn't stand it. It wasn't the money. He just felt like he was being taken advantage of. Brad was afraid to say anything to Terry, though. It was the only thing about Terry that he didn't like. He was afraid Terry would get mad and their friendship would be ruined.

Brad needs to communicate with Terry about how he feels. Chances are, Terry will understand the problem and change his behavior. If Brad allows the situation to continue, he will keep feeling angry and stressed. The friendship likely will be affected in the long run if the problem continues.

Have you ever felt nervous about talking with someone about a situation that is causing you stress? Here are some steps to follow.

Tell the person you want to talk with him or her about a problem. Say what the problem is and ask if it's a good time to talk. This prepares the person to deal with the problem instead of surprising him or her with it.

Explain the problem clearly and calmly. Tell how the problem affects you. For example, "When I pay for your meals all the time, I feel taken advantage of."

After you have explained the problem, listen to the other person's response.

Try to work out a solution to the problem together. You may want to think of some solutions ahead of time.

Sometimes people cannot agree on solutions to problems. Be prepared if the discussion doesn't turn out the way you expected or hoped. You always can try talking another time.

Sometimes just talking about problems can make them seem more manageable. Often teens think they are the only ones who feel overwhelmed by a problem or situation. In fact, most teens might be surprised to know that others share many of the same frustrations.

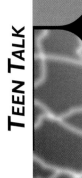

"I always end my day with a little time for myself. When I finish my homework at night, I read a fun book, listen to music, or drink a hot cup of tea. Sometimes it's hard to squeeze in the time for myself, but I think it really pays off. I feel a little grumpy if I skip my 'me time.'"—Dara, age 16

EMILIO, AGE 16

Some days Emilio feels like chucking it all. His coach keeps telling him to improve his drill times in football. He missed taking two tests when he was out with the flu. Now he has to study for the make-up tests. His job at the restaurant takes up all his spare time. He hasn't seen his girlfriend, Rose, in a week. He was griping to his friends in the cafeteria one day at school. Oliver said he felt the same way. Before they knew it, they all were laughing at the craziness in their life. Emilio felt a lot better after talking with his friends.

Ask for Help

Most people at some time in their life experience stress that seems unmanageable. It is not a sign of weakness to ask for help in dealing with stress. Check your phone book for listings for *Self-Help Groups, Counselors, Psychologists,* or *Psychiatrists.* Many professionals specialize in stress management. Be sure to check the Useful Addresses and Internet Sites section on page 62 of this book for organizations and other resources.

Points to Consider

Why do you think eating healthy foods can help a person fight off stress?

Have you ever had to tell a friend something about him or her that was bothering you? What happened?

Do you think sharing your feelings with others about being stressed is a stress reliever? Why or why not?

Angela is a teen with a lot of responsibilities. She goes to school, works, and takes care of her three younger brothers. Her dad works the night shift.

On a typical day, Angela experiences many stressors. Sometimes she feels out of control and unable to deal with them.

Angela can do many things to better manage her stress. She can plan ahead, eat a healthy diet, and ask for help. She can talk about her problems and make time for herself.

Chapter **6**

Angela's Day: How One Teen Deals With Stress

Angela is in 10th grade. She lives in an apartment with her father and three younger brothers. Her mom lives in another state. Angela goes to school and works in the afternoon. Her dad works the night shift.

Angela has many responsibilities. She gets her brothers ready for school and puts them to bed most nights. Sometimes she feels like she can't take any more stress. She feels likes she's going to snap.

Angela's Morning

Angela's alarm rings at 5:30 A.M. She groans and burrows under the covers. Finally she stumbles down the hall to the bathroom. She comes out of the shower still sleepy. She sits on the edge of her bed and stares at the clothes in her closet. Then she hears her brothers fighting in the other bedroom and rushes to get dressed.

"Quit fighting and get dressed," she yells. She hurries to the kitchen and starts making the boys' lunches. The dishes from last night's dinner are still in the sink. "How hard is it to do some dishes, Dad?" she mumbles aloud. Her brothers wander into the kitchen. Angela pours cereal and milk in three bowls and tells them to eat fast.

A few minutes later, her dad walks through the door. After a quick hello, Angela heads to the elevators. She makes it to the lobby before she realizes she left her backpack in the apartment. She runs back to get it, almost missing her bus.

More than 15 percent of young people who responded to a recent survey on stress said that everything stressed them out. Not one person surveyed said they had no stress.

Angela can barely keep her eyes open in her first hour class. Between classes, she stops at the vending machines for cola and chips. At lunch, she eats some cookies and drinks another cola. At her locker, another student bumps into her. "Watch it," Angela shouts at her. "You got a problem or something?" Later, she feels bad that she lost her temper. "What's wrong with me?" she thinks. "I feel like I hate everybody. I want the world to just go away and leave me alone."

Too Many Stressors

To Angela, life seems out of control. She yells at her brothers. She forgets things. She almost falls asleep in class. Sometimes Angela wishes she could trade her life for someone else's.

Angela could reduce some of the stress she feels in the morning by making a few changes. She could plan her day the night before. She could take care of her body by eating a healthy diet.

Plan Ahead

Angela makes lunch for her brothers every day. Often, she doesn't have time to make lunch for herself. That's why she grabs whatever is handy at the vending machine. Angela could save time in the morning by making her lunch and her brothers' lunches the night before. She also could save time if she decided what she was going to wear before she went to bed. If Angela spent time each evening planning for the next day, she might feel less stressed.

Stay Healthy

Like many teens, Angela eats on the run. She skips breakfast, has chips and a cola between classes, and grabs some cookies for lunch. She gets a quick energy boost from the sugary snacks, but her body needs more. It needs fruits, vegetables, protein, and plenty of water to stay healthy.

If Angela's body is healthy and strong, she may be better able to handle the stressors in her life. She could take care of her body by eating fruits, vegetables such as carrot sticks and celery, and whole-grain bread. Eating a healthy breakfast and lunch could give Angela the fuel she needs to get through the day.

Angela's Evening

After school, Angela gets a ride with a friend to her job at a fast-food restaurant. Before she can take her first order, her supervisor, Darren, asks her to stay late. He wants her to train a new employee. "I can't stay late," said Angela. "I have to watch my brothers after my shift." Darren asks her to come to his office. He tells her that she *will* train the employee. Angela is angry, but she doesn't say anything to Darren. However, she complains about him to the other employees on her break.

"Learn to laugh. Humor is not a trick, not jokes. Humor is a presence in the world [that] shines on everybody." —Garrison Keillor, writer and humorist

At 8:00, Angela heads home with a bag of fast food. Her dad is watching TV. He grabs the food from Angela and eats in the chair. Angela gives her brothers some chicken and tosses the dishes in the sink. She tries to ignore the TV and her brothers as she reads her history assignment. "This isn't working," she says and slams the book shut. Her dad kisses her goodnight and heads out to meet friends before work.

"Let's go," Angela says to her brothers as she tries to give them a bath. They are tired and wound up. They argue and fight with Angela. She yells and screams at them. It takes her until 10:00 to get them into bed. By then, she is too tired to finish her assignments. She calls her friend Ceelie and they talk while Angela drinks another cola. Angela crawls into bed an hour later.

The Stress Continues

Like Angela, many teens go to school, have a part-time job, and care for other family members. They may feel like they never have any time left over for the things they want to do. To them, it may seem like they are always doing things for someone else. Angela's responsibilities make her feel angry and resentful sometimes. However, she could relieve some of the stressors in her life by asking for help. She also could try to solve problems by talking about them with others. Finally, Angela needs to make time for herself.

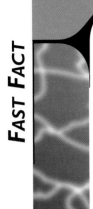

Ask for Help

Angela has a lot of responsibility for her brothers' care. Sometimes she feels like it's too much. Angela could talk with her father about helping her more. For example, she could ask that her father put the boys to bed a few evenings a week. She also could ask him to stay with the boys at night so she could study at the library. Together, they could work out a plan for sharing the housework and preparing meals.

Talk About Problems

Angela gets upset when her boss asks her to work late without telling her in advance. She sometimes feels her boss expects her to work harder and longer than the other employees. Doesn't she have enough stress in her life?

Talking about her concerns respectfully with her boss could help. Angela could explain to Darren how she feels when he asks her to work late at the last minute. She could explain why it is difficult for her to change her schedule. She might even suggest that Darren make her a crew leader so she could do training. She also might earn more money as a crew leader. Talking about the problems could make Angela feel less frustrated and angry. It could reduce the stress she feels about her job. She could even improve her relationship with Darren.

Take Time Out

Angela needs to make time to do things just for herself. She could set aside two hours one night a week to be with friends, exercise, or just be alone. On those days, she could plan to do homework at school or in the morning. She may have to work it out with her father, her brothers, and her boss. However, like all people, Angela needs a break from stress to feel her best physically and mentally.

Points to Consider

What are some ways you can organize your time to reduce the stress in your life?

Can you think of a time when you blew up at someone? How could you have handled the situation differently?

What are some things you can do to at the end of the day to feel less tense?

Glossary

adrenaline (uh-DREN-uh-lin)—epinephrine

bisexual (bye-SEK-shoo-wuhl)—sexual attraction to both males and females

chronic (KRON-ik)—continuing for a long time

cortisol (KOR-tuh-zol)—a hormone released in the body in response to stress

empathy (EM-puh-thee)—understanding the thoughts and feelings of others without having their experience

endorphins (en-DOR-finz)—chemicals produced in the brain that reduce pain and elevate mood

epinephrine (e-pi-NEF-rin)—a hormone released in the body in response to stress; epinephrine can increase heart rate and blood pressure.

eustress (YOO-stress)—a positive form of stress

heterosexual (het-er-oh-SEK-shoo-wuhl)—sexual attraction to a person of the opposite gender, or sex

homosexual (hoh-moh-SEK-shoo-wuhl)—sexual attraction to a person of the same gender, or sex

hormone (HOR-mohn)—a chemical produced by a gland or tissue; hormones enter the bloodstream and control various body processes.

immune system (i-MYOON SISS-tuhm)—the body system that protects against disease

psychiatrist (sye-KYE-uh-trist)—a medical doctor trained to diagnose and treat mental illness

psychologist (sye-KOL-uh-jist)—a person who provides testing and counseling to people with mental and emotional problems

stress (STRESS)—a person's physical and mental reaction to change

For More Information

Hageman, Frederick. *Making the Grade: How You Can Achieve Greater Success With Less Stress in School and Beyond.* Berkeley, CA: Rising Crescent Publishing, 1995.

Hipp, Earl. *Fighting Invisible Tigers.* Minneapolis: Free Spirit Publishing, 1995.

Peacock, Judith. *Anger Management.* Mankato, MN: Capstone Press, 2000.

Poesma, Frances. *Straight Talk About Today's Families.* New York: Facts on File, 1999.

Sprung, Barbara. *Stress.* Austin, TX: Raintree Steck-Vaughn, 1998.

Useful Addresses and Internet Sites

American Academy of Child and
Adolescent Psychiatry
3615 Wisconsin Avenue Northwest
Washington, DC 20016
1-800-333-7636
www.aacap.org

Canadian Mental Health Association (CMHA)
2160 Yonge Street, 3rd Floor
Toronto, ON M4S 2Z3
CANADA
www.cmha.ca

National Mental Health Association
1021 Prince Street
Alexandria, VA 22314
1-800-969-6642
www.nmha.org

Child and Family Canada
www.cfc-efc.ca
Online resources for a variety of health-related
topics

Family Doctor
http://familydoctor.org/handouts/278.html
Information about stress and how to deal with it

Health Education: Stress, Depression, Anxiety,
Drug Use
www.teachhealth.com/
Tells the medical basis of stress and
depression, with suggestions on how to fight
stress. Also in Spanish.

Teens and Stress
http://library.advanced.org/13561/
Gives information on causes, effects, and
prevention of stress for teens. Also in Spanish,
French, and German.

Wholistic Stress Control Institute
www.mindspring.com/~wholistic/teens_stress.
html
Defines stress, describes good and bad stress,
and gives tips for handling stress

Index

Index continued